HOW TO GET YOURSELF A SECOND LIFE

(A GUIDE FOR NEWBIES)

BY DANIEL JAMES HARRIS

Daniel J Harris

INTRODUCTION

Greetings!

My name is Wayne Rodnick Bohemia and I am one of the many inhabitant's of the online environment known as Second Life. I've been there since August 2006, and in the course of getting up to speed I've observed that while there are all kinds of different resources for people who are familiar with Second Life, there are very few for people who are just starting to figure it out, or even for people who haven't signed up yet. Admittedly, there are all kinds of helpful places for newbies within Second Life itself, but that can be a bit like learning to swim by getting chucked in the deep end. So I decided to create this little guide so that people who are just starting out or are thinking about it can get a feel for it so they can enter Second Life with a little more confidence.

Five Things To Do Before You Get Started in Second Life

Make sure you can actually play it.

This is *crucial*. Go to SecondLife.com and click on the little link "System Requirements" somewhere towards the bottom of the page. Read them with feeling. There are few things more frustrating than setting up an account, downloading the program and *then* finding out that you can't actually run it on your machine. I speak from experience on this one--if I hadn't had a chance to borrow someone else's computer and get hooked that way, I probably wouldn't be writing this page now.

Pick a name you can live with.

Previously, a new avatar could only input a first name and then had to pick from a list of surnames provided (a list which changed over time, which means you can, with some experience, gauge how old an avatar is by the surname they selected.) Now you can pick any otherwise untaken username and then change your 'Display Name' to anything you like, so it shouldn't matter what you pick, right? There's just one thing to consider when you do this, though. Even if you type in something like "Bob3254" and change your Display Name to "Awesome McCoolName", the only people who will see it are people who are using Viewers that are compatible with the Display Name feature. Users who are still using Viewer 1 or certain other alternate viewers, will see you as "Bob3254 Resident" and have no idea that you are, in fact, Awesome. Given that, it might be a good idea to put just a little bit of thought into the name you enter as your username, since for some that will be the only name they'll recognize.

Find a buddy.

The number one way to get the hang of Second Life in no time is to know somebody who is already there. It doesn't even have to be someone you know in person--when I first landed in Second Life, I met up with people I knew from the Duranie message boards. Ask around your usual Internet hangouts, or your meatspace social circle, and find out if anybody there is on Second Life. Find out what their avatar name is and ask if it's okay to contact them when you first arrive. Second Life is as much a social network as anything, and people are always happy to add new friends, especially if it's someone they already know from elsewhere.

Have a credit card or PayPal account handy.

While Second Life is currently available at no cost to you, you will find that your quality of life will go up quite a bit if you have a little extra money to spend. Setting up payment information doesn't even oblige you to use it, but that way it's there in case you need it. You can buy something like a thousand Lindens for the price of a fast food lunch, so it's not like you have to spend huge wads of cash. Also, if you decide that it's worth upgrading to a Premium membership, you'll be all lined up for it.

Have some kind of idea of what you'd like to try, but keep your options open.

It does help to have some sense of direction when you're wandering about. People come to Second Life for all kinds of things, from social chat to elaborate roleplay to the chance to stand around in a replica of the Sistine Chapel. Doing searches on things you're interested in may hook you up with what you're looking for. But, at the same time, don't get so hung up on one particular subculture or scene that you miss out on so many other aspects of Second Life. It's a big world. Feel free to explore it.

Ready to go? Download Second Life and have fun!

Five Things To Do Just After You Get Started in Second Life

Explore your tutorial experience.

Since where you land when you first log in keeps constantly changing, and Yours Truly can't really keep reincarnating with new alts to test the waters each time, this section is a big vague on the specifics. But when you log in to Second Life for the very first time, there is bound to be some kind of basic tutorial thingy to get you up to speed on things like walking around and changing your appearance.

As tempted as you may be to take the Eddie Izzard technojoy throw-out-the-instructions-and-figure-it-out-yourself approach, you will find that your experience will run more smoothly if you do all the silly little exercises so you can get a feel for how to make things go. Because you're likely to look even *more* silly if you go straight to the mainland and still don't know how to walk properly.

Find a decent place to call Home.

You first Home will probably be chosen at random. From that point forward, until you change it, that is the place you will return to when you hit the "Go Home" button on the Map, or where you will appear when you first log in with the "My Home" location selected as your entry point.

You can change the location of your Home by selecting "Set Home to Here" under the World menu. However, you can't set it just anywhere--it has to be either under land you own yourself, or at a spot called an Infohub. If you're not quite ready to buy land just yet, you can either settle for where you were dropped off (which might be fine) or you can find another Infohub and set your Home for there.

But how do you find another Infohub? The easiest way is the Search function. Click the Search button at the bottom of the screen, select the "Places" tab and type in "Infohub" and click the "Search" button just next to it. The various Infohubs will appear, ranked by traffic. (Hint: the highest traffic is not always the best place, because it also means that the place is more crowded and therefore prone to more lag.) Clicking on each entry will give you a picture and a description. Decide what looks good to you and click "Teleport" just underneath the description to go there and have a look. (I personally recommend the Isabel Infohub, which is right next to The Shelter, a little club that caters to those just starting out.) At any rate, when you find an Infohub you wouldn't mind returning to, set your Home there. You can always change it later if you find a better Infohub, or wind up buying your own place. (There are also certain Groups that own land that allow certain members the ability to set Home on that land, but that's a little too complicated to get into in a quick five things.)

Don't be afraid to tell people that you're a newbie.

At the very least, people will be more likely to forgive you for being clueless and less likely to suspect that you're somebody's alt. Many people will, in fact, be incredibly helpful and glad to take you by the hand and show you around. The most important thing is to *expect nothing*. Remember, people in SL aren't obliged to give you jobs, money, advice or the time of day just because you wandered within chat range of them. Just tell them that you're new and let them decide how they want to respond.

Better yet, find places that cater to newbies.

Once again, the Search function can be your friend. While a search on "Newbie" will land you all kinds of things--some useful, some less so-- an even better way to get oriented is to search the Events listings. You can search inworld by hitting the Search button and selecting the Events tab. In the little menu for "Category" select "Education". This will bring up a listing of scheduled Events that are classes. Some will be advanced classes in things you're just figuring out, but you will find a number of classes specifically for people who are just beginning. Note when they are and Teleport to them. Try to get there a little early, especially for classes of limited size, because sometimes the landing point isn't exactly where the classroom is.

By the way, you can also see the same Events listings (minus the Mature listings) on the secondlife.com website. You can even teleport directly from the website through the SLURL provided.

Take advantage of as many freebies as you can find.

Okay, maybe not every single freebie--otherwise your inventory will explode to ridiculous proportions in a short period of time. But when you're just starting out, having some halfway decent hair, skin and clothes will do wonders to get rid of that newbie look. Freebies are a good way to get a feel for what's available and what's worth spending money on before you graduate to actual cash money. Just do a search for "freebies" in the Places tab and you'll find loads of stuff right off the bat. (I recommend Vienna Freebies and Sarah Nerd's Freebie Paradise for starters.) There are also established shops that provide free sample hair and skin to avatars less than 30 days old--if you can find them, grab them.

Some 'freebies' will require a payment of L$1, but given that a Linden is less than a penny (the exchange rate is roughly 250 Lindens to the US Dollar) it's close enough to free. You might be able to grab a few Lindens from a Money Tree if you remain determined to spend absolutely no cash money on anything in Second Life.

How Do I . . . ?

Second Life allows you do to all sorts of amazing things, but it's not necessarily obvious to the beginner how to do them. Plus, many things can be done in more than one way. This page is a partial list of such things for the benefit of the complete newbie, from the simple to the more complicated. As of this writing, the list is in order of when I think of them, and I hope to add to it regularly.

So, for those who are trying to figure out "How do I . . . "

. . . walk around?

You'd think this one would be a no-brainer, but judging by the number of day-old avatars who have trampled me trying to figure it out, maybe not.

Movement is directed by the arrow keys on your keyboard. Up moves you forward, down moves you back, and the left and right keys turn your avatar accordingly. Releasing the keys will bring your avatar to a stop (unless you're on enough of a slope that the physics engine kicks in and causes your avatar to stumble forward until it hits level ground.)

Your movement can be blocked by solid prims and other avatars. This can sometimes be confusing when you've just arrived somewhere and the place isn't completely finished rendering, since a wall that hasn't yet appeared on your screen can be seen through, but not walked through. (Some prims are set as "phantom" so they can be moved through, and they're usually set as translucent as a hint.)

By the way, if you *do* bump into people, a simple "excuse me" can go a long way. Just sayin'.

. . . fly?

On most keyboards, the "Page Up" and "Page Down" keys will allow you to fly. Pressing "Page Up" again will lift you a little bit higher and the "Page Down" key will cause you to descend. If, like, me, you're on a laptop and said keys are also the arrow keys, you'll need to hold down whatever key is needed to cause it to perform that function (the "fn" key on mine, it may vary by laptop.) Otherwise, the arrow keys will cause you to move forward, backward and turn as they would if you were on the ground.

"Free Flight", for lack of a better term, is slightly limited in how high and how fast you can go. Also, certain parcels of land will have properties set to disallow flight--you can fly over them if you're passing through, but if you land, you're stuck. You can fly a bit higher and faster if you have a scripted object active on your person--whether it's a flying vehicle, rocket boots or a "flight feather" which you can wear.

. . . teleport somewhere?

Teleportation is the number one means of travel in Second Life. As such, there are lots of different ways to do it.

Landmarks are the main way. They're sort of the Second Life equivalent of webpage bookmarks. You can set one up almost anywhere by pressing the little star in your browser window thingy at the top of your screen. More often, you'll pick them up from people, places and things that give them to you. It will show in in your inventory as a globe with the name of the place next to it. Double click and and you'll be asked if you really want to Teleport there. If you do, click "Teleport."

If you look at the map, you can also select Landmarks from a menu, but they have a bad habit of accumulating and getting hard to follow, for some reason. You can also teleport from the map by double-clicking on the map on the place you'd like to be. If you're allowed, you'll teleport there.

You can also get a teleport from someone else . . . or give one. To teleport someone to where you are, pull up their Profile (see below) and click "Teleport". (If the button is grayed out, they're probably not around to offer a Teleport to.)

If they're a Friend of yours, you can also offer a teleport from your Contacts list. Just click People and click the "My Friends" tab. Select the name in the list of friends and click the "Teleport" button. If they're offline, the "Teleport" button will be greyed out.

A message will pop up, which usually defaults to "Join me in [wherever you are]. This is what they'll see when they get the notice that you're offering a teleport. You can rewrite it, if you like, but most people just leave it as is.

And, of course, if somebody teleports you, you'll get a message asking to accept or decline. Hit "Teleport" and you'll be teleported to where that person is.

. . . talk to people?

If you want to talk to the whole room, just click where it says "Click here to chat" in the lower left corner, type what you want to say, and hit Enter. While you're typing, your avatar will usually do a little hands-in-midair thing (as if typing on an invisible keyboard) and clickety-tappity sounds will be heard. If you hear the clickety-tappity sounds and you're *not* typing anything, it means that somebody else in earshot is typing. What you say (and what other people say) will appear on the lower left of your screen and gradually fade out depending on how you set your preferences.

If you miss something, click the arrow at the end of the chat space to bring up the chat log. If you want to talk to an individual and not the whole room, you can send that person an Instant Message (IM). Which, of course, brings you to the question "how do I . . ."

. . . send an IM to someone?

If the person is in the room, you can right-click on either the avatar or the name that's floating above their head and select "IM" from the menu that pops up. (You can use Command-click if you're a single button Macintoshy person like me, and just assume the same when I say "right-click" from this point forward.) The Communicate screen will pop up, this time with a tab for the person you're IMing. Type what you want to say in the chat line just above the tab and hit Enter. What you said will show up in the window above. If the person responds, you'll see a line that says "[avatar name] is typing..." (sort of the IM equivalent of the clickety-tappity) at the top of the chat window and then when they hit Enter, what they wrote will appear in the window.

If the person is not in the room, you can still IM them. Heck, they don't even have to be inworld at the time! Neat, huh? If you have established the person as a Friend, you can do it from your My Friends list (as above.) Just click the "IM" button (or double-click on the name.) A new tab will appear, proceed as above. If you're able to see the Online status of the Friend, it will let you know if the person happens to be offline. Type what you need and the moment you hit Enter you'll get the message "User not online - message will be stored and delivered later." Note that it will tell you this *every single time you hit Enter* as long as the person is offline. When the person arrives inworld, they will get the IMs that have accumulated while away. It's my understanding that such IMs are "capped" after a certain number, so try not to ramble too much.

If the individual is *not* on your Friends list, you can pull up that person's Profile (we'll get to how to do that in a moment) and click the "IM" button. You won't find out if they're on or offline until you hit Enter (though if the "Teleport" button on their profile is greyed out, chances are, they ain't.)

. . . pull up a Profile?

Somehow I figured you'd be asking that. There are a number of ways.

As with IMing, if the person is in the room with you, you can right-click on their avatar or their name and select "Profile" from the menu.

If the person is one of your Friends, you can click their name in your My Friends list (see above) and then click the "Profile" button.

If the person is not on your list and not in the room, their Profile can still be obtained through the wonders of the Search function. Put in the name of the person you're looking for in the Search in the upper right of your screen and the nearest matches will appear (including, presumably, the person you're looking for.) Click on the name and then click "Details" to get to the Profile.

Ways To Get Inworld: Second Life Viewers

The way inworld is through a program known as a viewer. Viewers, much like browsers, do roughly the same job but may have slight variations in the exact instructions. For example, following the exact instructions to add a bookmark in Internet Explorer will just confuse you terribly if you're working in Safari.

This site was originally put together under the previous iteration of the official Second Life viewer but is in the process of updated to reflect the changes in Viewer 2, which can be downloaded at SecondLife.com. For simplicity, tutorials on this site will refer to the most recent versions of the SL Viewer (depending on how quickly I can get updates up!)

Since the source code has been generously put out to be tinkered with, there are a wide number of viewers available to access Second Life with. A comprehensive list can be found on the Second Life Wiki. Linden Lab has instituted a Third Party Viewer policy that places certain requirements on viewers for them to be officially accepted, so you might do best to pick one of those out. Just keep in mind that what you read here may not match what you see on your personal viewer.

Tips For Noobs #1: How To See What You're Doing

Your first fumbling steps in Second Life will almost inevitably be with an exquisite view of the back of your avatar's head.

But what if you want to see yourself from the front?

Since Second Life is designed as a visual environment, it really does help to be able to *see* things. Thus, your experience can be enhanced greatly by mastering the wonders of the camera controls.

"Camera", in this case, refers to the "point of view" that you view the world from on your screen. The camera will follow whatever you have selected as its point of focus. By default, the point of focus is your avatar, so that wherever your avatar goes, the camera shall follow.

The camera can be moved around this point of focus through a couple of different means.

At the bottom of your screen, you should see a button labeled 'View'. Pressing this reveals a series of options.

The button with the little arrow circling around is the Orbit Zoom Pan view.

The set of arrows on the left (in the circle) is the orbit controls. The left and right arrows will move the camera around your point of focus and the up and down arrows will tilt the camera up over or down below it. The plus/minus slider in the middle will zoom the camera in and out. The arrows on the right (in the square) control the Pan view. This will send the camera up, down, left or right, depending on which arrow you press.

The little eyeball brings up a series of preset camera positions.

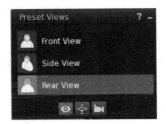

These have been helpfully labeled Front View, Side View and Rear View. However, these camera positions are actually relative to *where the point of focus was last*. If you've been messing about with the camera controls and then switch to these presets, you may find that Front View will end up being Rear View or Side View, depending on where the camera was pointing at the time. If this happens (indeed any time your camera winds up in a confusing place) simply press the Escape key, which should bring the point of focus back to just behind your avatar.

The little camera brings up the two Camera Modes.

Object view will turn your pointer into a sort of magnifying glass with a plus on it and clicking on something in this mode will change the point of focus to what you click on. Clicking and dragging will also move the camera in, out or around, depending on which direction you drag. (Forward will go in and backward will zoom out. Left and right will move the camera around the point of focus.)

Mouselook makes the point of focus visible as a tiny square with a sort of crosshair space in the center. Move your mouse to move the crosshair and the camera will follow. Even though you can't see your avatar, you can still move, though the left and right keys will move your avatar from side to side rather than turning. Mouselook is principally used for shooting games, as the crosshairs signal to scripted objects where one's 'aim' is. You'll notice Mouselook also has the helpful reminder to "Press ESC to return to World View" at the bottom of the screen, as it can be triggered accidentally (by hitting the letter "M" when chat isn't active) and can be awfully disorienting if unexpected.

All of these menus are pretty much 'training wheels' to get you used to manipulating the camera. Once you get the hang of them, there are far simpler keyboard commands to work with. (As a matter of fact, if you use these keyboard controls while the Orbit Zoom Pan control is still on your screen, you'll see the corresponding controls highlight as if you're clicking them!)

- Holding down the Alt key while using the arrow keys will arc the camera around on the left and right keys and zoom the camera in and out on the up and down keys. (Up will zoom in, down will zoom out.)
- Holding down the Control and Alt keys will have the same effect with the left and right arrow keys, but the up and down keys will tilt the camera up and down accordingly. (Note to Mac users: use the Control key, not the Command key, since the - Command key is already on duty as your substitute left mouse button.)
- Control, Alt and Shift all held together at once (a bit cumbersome, but possible) will set the arrow keys to track left, right, up and down (in the same way the Pan view does.)

PS--those of you with rotating wheelie things on your mouses will find that the wheelie will also serve to zoom in and out. I can't tell you much about that, 'cos I'm a MacBook person, but there you are.

So, now you can see your avatar from all possible angles. Pretty neat, huh? But what if you want to focus your camera on something else?

The point of focus can be changed at any time (or even back to yourself) by Alt-clicking on whatever you want to look at. So if you want to look at a sign, you can Alt-click on the sign and angle the camera so you can see it clearly. If you want to observe a statue, you can Alt-click on the statue and look all around it. You can even Alt-click on other avatars in your view, though this can be very disorienting if they get up and walk somewhere else, as the camera will follow right after them. Once again, if your camera gets dragged somewhere and you need to retrieve it, hitting Escape will bring the point of focus back to you.

If you want even finer focus of your camera, you can combine the key combinations mentioned above with clicking and dragging.

- Alt-dragging will move the camera around as you move left and right, and zoom the camera in and out as you move it up and down.
- Control-Alt-dragging will also move the camera around at left and right, and tilt the camera up and down as you move the mouse up and down.
- Shift-Control-Alt dragging will track the camera in whatever direction you move the mouse.

Now go and see what there is to see!

Tips For Noobs #2: How To Dress Yourself, Part One: Clothing Layers

Contrary to the impression you may have gotten about Second Life, avies do not wander about naked as a general rule. (Since simple clothing can easily be conjured up in the Appearance settings, there's really no excuse for it, either.) Clothing items come in layers that cover the avie in specific ways and overlap accordingly.

My lovely assistant, Beginning Thursday, shall demonstrate.

The skin of the avie might be considered the very bottom layer. Some skins are even modest enough to include underwear directly on the body, much the way late-model Barbie dolls now come with permanent panties. Beginning is wearing a standard-issue Girl Next Door skin (available in the Library section of your Inventory) which she has tweaked to her preferences in the Appearance settings.

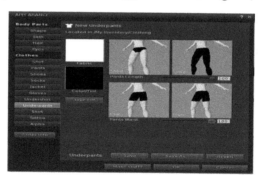

Any item of clothing can be added via the Appearance settings. For purposes of this demonstration, all the length sliders have been maxed to show the full coverage of each layer on the avatar.

The Underpants layer covers the legs from waist to ankle. It can be adjusted for length, but not for looseness.

Similarly, the Undershirt layer covers the torso, arms and part of the neck and can only be adjusted at the edges. The body-hugging aspects of these layers make them popular for things like tattoos, battle scars and, obviously, undergarments.

The Glove and Socks layers cover the hands and feet and a certain portion of the arms and legs. They also cover the Underpants and Undershirt layers in the event of overlap.

The Shoes layer covers the same area as the Socks layer but additionally forms the feet of the avatar into a shoe like shape, depending on how the item is set in the Appearance settings. Most prim shoes come with a set of 'system shoes' that will squish the feet into the optimal shape to fit into the prim shoes without poking out. (Prim shoes will be discussed in Part Two: Attachments.)

The Shirt and Pants layers cover the same area as the Undershirt and Underpants layers but can also be adjusted to 'flare' at the cuffs and be slightly looser around the avatar instead of body hugging. (The results are not always aesthetically pleasing, and thus the the 'looseness' adjustments are used sparingly by the more image-conscious.)

The Jacket layer covers the Shirt layer and a portion of the Pants layer. It has no looseness adjustments of its own other than 'wrinkles', but will follow the contours of any Shirt layer underneath it. (If there is no Shirt layer, it will take on the contours of the skin as the Undershirt layer does.)

And, finally, the much-maligned Skirt layer, which lies slightly outside of the lower body even at its tightest and sometimes drives avies to push the Appearance sliders for their rear end all the way to the minimum in order to avoid Does This Make My Butt Look Big Syndrome.

The newest version of the Second Life viewer (Viewer 2) has introduced two extra layers, which I will demonstrate here. Note that some alternate viewers may not be able to 'see' these layers.

The tattoo layer covers the entire skin area and lies 'between' the skin and the undershirt layer. As mentioned before, most tattoos went on the undershirt layer previously (and many for purchase still do.)

The Alpha layer applies transparency to the avatar mesh. As demonstrated here, it will cause clothing to disappear, but prim attachments remain visible. Partial alphas can be used for things like peg legs, robotic arms and headless horsemen.

When wearing clothes acquired from elsewhere (as you will often do) you need to keep the Layer system in mind for a couple of reasons. One, of course, is knowing what layer covers another layer. The other is that each layer only allows for one item of clothing at a time. If you have a neat tattoo as your Undershirt layer and then wear a bra on that Undershirt layer, there goes your tattoo. (Some designers are aware of this conundrum and will provide the same outfit in multiple layers so you can mix and match with other items in your Inventory more freely.)

There are a number of ways to put on clothes in Second Life. The quickest and easiest way is to double-click on the item in your Inventory. The name of it will be bolded and the word "(worn)" added to the details. (Incidentally, searching on "worn" in your Inventory will bring up everything with 'worn' in the description--this includes everything that you are currently wearing, but keep in mind it will also include anything with 'worn' in the name, so note which items are bolded to get a feel for what you're actually wearing.) Depending on lag, it might take a moment for the item to make it onto your body, so try to be patient. Double-clicking again will not reverse the process--you will need to right-click the item and select "Take Off" to remove it.

You can also drag the item of clothing onto your body from the Inventory window for roughly the same effect. This technique is best for selecting multiple items (using Shift-select to select a row of items or Ctrl-select to pick out noncontiguous items) and dragging them all to your avatar at once.

Some will advocate placing a favourite outfit in a folder and dragging the folder onto your avatar. While this technically works, it has some hazards. It will not only add the items in the folder, it will remove any removable items *not* in the folder. This includes any prim or HUD attachments, which might leave you bald and walking funny. Seriously. (Again, we will speak more of prim attachments in Part Two.) A better method is to right-click the folder and select "Add To Outfit", which will allow you to leave on whatever you had on at the time that isn't on the same layers as the existing outfit. ("Replace Outfit" is the equivalent of dragging the folder on, right down to the bald-and-walking-funny side effects.)

Most items of clothing will have relatively self-explanatory icons to indicate what layer it covers. Extremely old items of clothing will have an odd flat shirt-looking thing regardless of what layer and even older ones will have something like a body icon. (Icons are not pictured here, as they are prone to evolution and dependent upon which viewer you are using.)

However, once you go from clothing layers into prim attachments, everything ends up looking like a box in your inventory. In the next part of this tutorial, we'll get into the fine art of How To Wear Boxes And Look Good Doing It.

Tips For Noobs #3: How To Dress Yourself, Part Two: Attachments

It is an admitted limitation of Second Life that there is only so much you can do to shape the avatar mesh into a pleasing form. Avatar hair is a weird and clumpy mass, avatar shoes deform the feet all too obviously and don't get some people started on the system skirt. Fortunately, thanks to the wonders of modern primitive technology, the avatar has many more options for enhancing one's appearance.

Objects in Second Life can be attached to the avatar at a number of bodily attachment points. (The exact number being thirty, in case you wondered.)

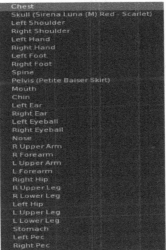

Just as each clothing layer can only hold one item at a time, each attachment point can only hold one object. While this has its advantages (you didn't particularly *want* to wear two shoes on the same foot, did you?) it can sometimes result in some hard choices to make, particularly when dealing with the lesser-used attachment points, which are sometimes used for 'internal' objects like Animation Overrides and Titlers.

To wear an Object, select it in your Inventory and click the Wear button. (You can also right-click the object and select "Wear.")

The Object will attach to the last attachment point it found itself at. If it hasn't previously been attached to an avatar, it will default to the right hand. (This can be a touch embarrassing if it turns out, for example, that the hair you just bought is still in a box that needs to be unpacked, but given that the previous default point was the *head*, this is a bit of an improvement.)

A few designers are helpful enough to let you know in the name of the item where it is destined to attach to. Most, however, do not, so when wearing a new item, it's generally a good idea to check and see what attachment point it's been hooked into, so when mixing and matching outfits you don't wind up missing the back of your sculpted trench coat because your wings got in the way.

As mentioned in the previous lesson, any item you wear (be it clothing, prim attachment or body part) will be bolded in your inventory and have "(worn)" next to the name. If it is a prim attachment, it will also tell you *where* it is worn, (such as "(worn on skull)" for prim hair.)

You can also change an item from one attachment point to another, though it can be a touch tricky because of the quirks of the attachment points. As always, Beginning Thursday will demonstrate for you.

First off, before doing any adjustments to attachments, you will need a posing stand - You can find one at most clothing stores in-world and they are normally available free of charge.

Beginning is wearing a lovely lighted pink bracelet which has been set to attach to the Right Forearm attachment point. (You can get one yourself for free, inworld at Social Butterfly.)

She would like to shift it to the Left Forearm. Step one is simple enough--right-click the bracelet in Inventory and select Attach To > L Forearm.

Unfortunately, the result is a bracelet embedded in her elbow, which isn't quite the effect we had in mind here. Therefore, the next step is to right-click the bracelet and select "Edit." This brings up our friend the Edit window and allows us to reposition the bracelet.

First, use the arrows to get the bracelet to the wrist. In this case, grabbing the green arrow (X axis) and pulling it down works perfectly. In other cases, you may need to fiddle with the other axes as well. It's generally a good idea to confine yourself to manipulating one axis at a time when you're just getting the hang of things.

Next, select Rotate on the edit window (or hold down the Control key.) This will change the arrows to three circles that designate rotation.

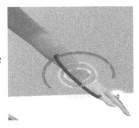

Click and drag on the circle so it will turn in the direction you want. In this case, we want the blue one (Z axis.) When you select one, the other two planes will disappear so you can adjust accordingly.

Release and voila! The bracelet is turned to fit on the wrist instead of inside it,

Right-click and select "Detach" to remove.

From that point forward, each time you click "Wear", the object will attach to the point you left it at.

If the object in question is copyable, you might consider making a 'backup' before fiddling with other attachment points or readjusting where it sits on your avatar. (To make a copy of an item, right-click the object and select "Copy" then pick a folder in your Inventory to keep it in, right-click the folder and select "Paste." If it won't let you select "Copy" this means the permissions have been set to non-copy.)

HUD attachments (Heads Up Display--objects that attach to your screen rather than your avatar) are a slightly different kettle of prims, but we'll get to those in a future tutorial. In the meantime, get out there and enjoy looking fabulous!

The SLexicon

Terms and abbreviations that are relatively common to Second Life.

AFK: Away From Keyboard.

Alt: An additional account in Second Life. The reason why thirteen million Residents (at last count) doesn't necessarily add up to thirteen million people.

Animation: The movements your avatar makes, basically. The 'default' animations are the movements your avatar makes as a matter of course. An animation is a sort of programmed sequence that can be activated to make your avatar move or pose in a specific way. They can be 'played' by double-clicking on them in your Inventory, or they can be placed in Gestures or scripted objects and activated that way.

AO: Animation Override. The default animations for things like walking are a bit clumsy, so various devices that attach to the avatar (sometimes as a bodily attachment, other times as a HUD) and play more graceful animations are quite common. You can get many for free and more elaborate ones can be purchased.

Attachment: An object that is 'worn' on the avatar, generally by right-clicking it on your Inventory and selecting "Wear". There are a number of different 'attachment points' on the body of the avatar, but only one attachment can go on a given point at a given time. Sometimes this is fine, if you want to change your hair or boots or something you can just add the new attachment and the old one will automatically detach to make room for it; other times, you'll find you need to choose between the groovy chain piercing and the groovy sunglasses, because they're both set to attach to the nose.

Avatar: The 'body' that you use to interact with others in Second Life.

Avie: Abbreviation for 'avatar'. Also spelled Avi, AV.

Away Mode: If your avatar is left inactive for long enough, it slumps forward as if dozing and the word "(Away)" appears next to the name. (The time elapsed is determined by how you set your preferences.) The moment you tap a key or move your mouse, the avatar will "wake up" again.

BIAB: Business In A Box. A box of full-perms merchandise that is resold to others. The notion is that you can set up a shop and sell the items to people. The reality is that the BIABs themselves wind up sold and resold for cheaper and cheaper prices until they're practically worthless. Additionally, the merchandise within is often so old and so crap that no sensible person would spend good Lindens on them, (particularly when they can buy the whole store for the price of a BIAB) to say nothing of the fact that selling items you didn't create without the creator's knowledge or consent is not regarded highly in the world of Second Life. BIABs are probably best purchased for one's personal use, as a way of obtaining a large number of full-perm items to experiment with and see how they're made.

Bling: Jewellery--or indeed, just about anything--that gives off flashing light particles at regular intervals. The charm of it seems to wear off the longer one has been around.

Bot: An avatar operated by a program instead of a person. Bots are controversial because most of the programs that run them are created to 'game' the system in some way, such as 'landbots' that scan for land offered for sale and rush in to buy it the instant a parcel is placed for sale at a price under a certain threshold. The current policy appears to be that bots are permitted as long as they don't do anything that would get a person-operated avatar kicked out if they did the same.

Camping: As mentioned in The Highly Opinionated FAQ at the rear of this book, camping is a way to make a few Lindens by sitting in one place and boosting traffic statistics. The practice was recently banned by Linden Lab, but there may still be places that haven't been obliterated yet.

Chat: The main means of communication in SL. You can also give commands to scripted objects through the chat, often by using a different channel than the main one.

Channel: Objects can be scripted to 'listen' and respond to typed instructions. A channel enables one to type instructions at an object without everybody in the room hearing, and also can relieve the object from having to keep track of everything said in open chat. So if you have a lamp that's scripted to listen to channel 7, you could type "/7 on" or "/7 off" to turn it on and off, and not worry about it blinking on and off any time somebody says the words "on" or "off" in casual conversation.

Emote: A way to state something in chat in the form of a sentence, by preceding it with /me. For example, if I type "I am very confused." into the chat line, the chat that appears will read "Wayne Bohemia: I am very confused." If I type "/me is very confused." the chat that appears will be "Wayne Bohemia is very confused." without the little colon in between.

Flexi: Short for flexible. Certain types of prims can be given 'flexible path' settings that allow them to bend and react to movement. Flexi prims are popular for things like prim hair and prim skirts.

Gesture: A preset series of actions triggered by a chat command, generally starting with a slash. A gesture can be set to play a sound, type preset text into the chat line, play an animation, or all three. There are a series of preset gestures that come with SL, and you can create new ones and pass those gestures on to others to use.

Grid: A collection of servers that holds the information that comprises the world of Second Life. In addition to the Main Grid, there is also the Preview Grid (or Beta Grid) which allows one to test the next generation of server code and the Teen Grid, for 13-17 year olds.

Griefer: The SL equivalent of a "troll" on a message board--someone who makes a deliberate effort to abuse other avatars and disrupt things, sometimes to the point of causing sims to crash completely. As with trolls, the easiest way to deal with them is to ignore them until they get bored and go away--the more you react, the more likely it is they'll try to provoke you even further.

Group: While group with a small G could describe any gathering of avatars, Group with a large G specifies a particular feature of Second Life. A Group can be formed for the price of L$100 and requires a minimum of two people in it. Groups have a number of features such as a IM channel for Group members, the ability for certain people to send out Notices for members to receive and even certain land permissions depending how the Group is set up. Each Resident can belong to a maximum of 25 Groups.

Hovertext: Text that, well, hovers over an object through the magic of the llSetText function in LSL. Hovertext becomes part of the prim's properties *even if the script is subsequently removed* so getting rid of or changing hovertext requires modifying or replacing the script.

HUD: Heads-Up Display. This is an object, usually scripted, that attaches to your screen rather than to your avatar. HUDs are often used to control other scripted objects, providing an additional "push-button" interface for it.

IM: Instant Message. This is the way one chats with someone without the rest of the grid overhearing. It can be used long distance, or even if the avatar is in the same room with yours, as long as the other Resident is logged in. You can also send IMs to people who aren't logged in at the time and they'll receive them upon their return (though if there are too many messages waiting, they run the risk of getting 'capped' and not being delivered.)

Inworld: The state of being logged into Second Life. ("I'll be inworld this evening.")

Island: This is land that is bought from Linden Lab and run directly by the landowner. (US$1,000 to start, US$295 per month to maintain. Yes, that's US dollars, not Linden dollars. (I dare you to buy one today!)These parcels are separated from the Mainland and the owner has more control over it than one would by buying a Mainland parcel. The owner can 'sell' the land to others, but it's more of a sublet arrangement than an actual purchase--no tier fees are paid directly to Linden Lab other than the monthly fee that the landowner pays. Most landowners have some kind of tier payment arrangement with those who 'buy' land on their Island (so they don't lose money and sometimes even turn a profit) and often have covenants that restrict what kind of things you can build on that land.

Lag: Information overload that slows things to a crawl in SL. The causes of lag are various, the results inevitably frustrating. The better your bandwidth and your system, the fewer problems you'll have with it, but there has yet to be a way to eliminate it completely.

Limo: This is an odd bit of slang for "teleport", so instead of saying "Send me a TP" you ask "Send me a limo." Often used when announcing events--"IM Somebody Avatar for a limo!"

LSL: Linden Scripting Language. The programming language used in scripts to make objects do things.

Mainland: Land owned by Linden Lab on the 'continents'. Land here can only be purchased by Residents with a Premium membership, but there are no covenants and few restrictions on what one can do with the land.

Neko: An otherwise human-shaped avatar wearing cat ears and a tail. (Whiskers are apparently optional.) Nekos sometimes also use feline-themed Gestures to do things like meow, purr and lick themselves. It can be seen as anything from a fashion statement to a lifestyle, depending on who you talk to. The term comes from the Japanese word for "cat."

Object: As atoms link together to form molecules, so prims link together to form objects. A single prim can also, by itself, be an object.

Particle: A temporarily generated texture, used for effects like snowflakes, candle flames, fireworks, flashing lights and the occasional alien invasion. Particles emit from prims that are scripted to generate them.

Partner: *verb:* To establish a relationship between two avatars via the Second Life Partnership Page. *noun:* An avatar so partnered. Avatars have the name of their partner visible and linked in their Profile. While ostensibly the equivalent of marriage in SL, what the partnership means is really up to the Residents in question--some business partners, for example, use partnering to designate their business relationship. The majority of the time, however, a partnership implies a romantic connection of some sort and a "wedding industry" has grown up around it. A partnership costs L$20 to establish (with the costs split evenly at L$10 for each avatar) and L$25 to dissolve (with the costs of dissolution being borne entirely by the Resident who requests it.)

Perms: Short for "permissions"--each object, texture and article of clothing that one creates can have different permissions set for subsequent owners. Modify (usually abbreviated as Mod) means that one can modify the item (changing the sleeve length on a shirt, for example). Copy means, obviously, that you can make unlimited copies of it. Transfer (usually abbreviated as Trans) means that you can give the item to someone else. Note that if an item is set to Transfer, it also means that it can be set for sale by the new owner. An item that has all three options checked is known as "full perms". An item can be set as either non-copy or non-trans, but not both.

Pie Menu: The circular menu that pops up where you right-click (or Command-click, if you're a Mac person) on a person, place or thing. What options appear on the menu depends on what you end up right-clicking on. If you didn't mean to click on what you did, clicking in the center will close the menu without incident.

Poseball: A prim scripted to trigger an animation when sat upon. There's no particular reason it *has* to be a ball, other than it's what people are used to. Poseballs on furniture place the avatar in a certain position, for example, and similar balls can be found on dance floors in matched pairs, to allow two avatars to dance together by each sitting on one of the balls. (They're traditionally tinted pink for the lady and blue for the gentleman in ballroom dance type animations.) To use one, right-click on the poseball and select "sit" (sometimes the script will replace with word with "dance" or whatever else the animation will have you do.) When you want to stop, click the "Stand Up" button towards the bottom of your screen.

Posing stand: A scripted prim, usually in the form of a platform, that will hold the avatar in the arms-out "Editing Appearance" position when you right-click and select "Stand." This comes in handy for making adjustments on prim attachments, since the avatar will tend to move around a bit otherwise. Much like the poseball, clicking the "Stand Up" button at the bottom of the screen will cause the avatar to hop off.

Prim: The basic "building block" of physical objects (as opposed to avatars) in SL.

Prim Hair: Hair made from prims that is worn as an attachment as opposed to 'avatar hair' that is shaped by the Appearance settings. Prim hair is generally built with lots of prims, many on flexible settings.

Prim Limit: Since each prim takes a certain amount of computer memory to render, the folks at Linden Lab place a limit on the number of prims that can be placed in a given amount of land. A standard issue 512 square meter plot of land, for example, holds 117 prims. Owners of Islands are given a certain number of prims for the entire sim, and will sometimes distribute them in such a way so a larger or smaller amount of prims can be placed within a given plot of land than a similar mainland plot. Note that this limit only applies to things that are physically on the land and not things that are attached to avatars on the land.

Prim Skirt: Much like prim hair, a skirt made from prims (usually flexi) that is worn as an attachment as opposed to the skirt created in Appearance settings.

Resident: A unique, named account in Second Life. Note that a given flesh-and-blood individual can own and operate more than one Resident. (See also alt.) Sometimes abbreviated as resi. The word avatar is sometimes used to refer to a Resident, but two words are not precisely interchangeable, as a given Resident can change from one body to another and the word avatar more precisely describes that body.

Rez: 1. To create a new object in SL. ("Rez a cylinder.") 2. To drag an object out of your inventory into the world, generally by placing it on the ground. ("Rez the chair you just bought.") 3. To first appear on the screen. Since Second Life is constantly changing, each time you enter a new location, it takes time to download, much like a webpage. Waiting for objects, avatars, etc. to appear on your screen is known as "rezzing." The term purportedly comes from the movie *Tron*.

RL: Abbreviation for "Real Life"--the life that belongs to the person at the keyboard as opposed to the avatar on the screen. (Some people use the abbreviation FL for "First Life", but this is less common because it also happens to be the United States Postal Service abbreviation for the state of Florida.)

RP: Abbreviation for Roleplay. Role playing games, are, of course, nothing new to the Internet, and Second Life provides a platform for all kinds of roleplay scenarios to unfold. The settings and rules will vary by each group, though one rule that should apply to any civilized avie is "please don't interfere if you're not playing."

Sandbox: A plot of land that allows and encourages anybody to build stuff on it (as long as you take what you've built with you when you're done.)

Script: A sequence of code written in LSL. Scripts are placed inside prims in order to make them do stuff.

Scripting: The act of coding a script. The syntax is reportedly similar to C, for you geek types.

Sculpted Prim: Also known as a sculptie, a sculpted prim is a prim that has its shape defined by a specialized texture (a "sculpt texture") that maps the spatial coordinates of the prim's surface using the Red, Blue and Green values of the image. These textures can be created through plug-ins for various 3D programs, and through programs specifically designed to create sculpt textures. Since the textures that define the shape have to download just like any other texture does when it reaches your screen, sculpties will often have a weird blobby quality when you're first rezzing in a new location.

(Note that the texture that *defines* the surface and the visible texture *on* the surface are two different textures, unless blurry psychedelic colors are really your thing.) Sculpties allow one to do elaborate constructions with fewer prims, but the level of detail can vary by what sort of program you use and how well you make use of it.

Silks: Silks are generally scanty outfits with flexiprim 'veils' at various attachment points. They originated in the Gorean roleplaying subculture but the term has since spread into the mainstream of SL.

Sim: Short for "simulator", this is actually shorthand for a 256x256 meter (65,536 m²) region that land in SL is subdivided into.

Skybox: A building, usually residential, that hovers far above the surface with no visible (or invisible) means of support. Skyboxes take advantage of the fact that, within Second Life, Newton's Law of Universal Gravitation is more like Newton's Supplemental Rule, which object must 'opt-in' to via ticky box. Skyboxes provide a certain modicum of privacy, since they usually occupy an altitude that cannot be reached by unaided flight. (Teleporation is the usual means of entry.) Some have spectacular views, while others may just have views of . . . other skyboxes. Note that they can be rezzed above any land that allows building, must to the surprise of some landowners who found skyboxes hovering far above their houses . . . and consuming their prim limit.

SL: Abbreviation for "Second Life."

Stream: Streaming music is, of course, not a feature unique to Second Life. Internet radio stations of all kinds have flourished because of it. Second Life has the option to stream music (and video) on a given parcel of land. You can, for example, set your land to play your favorite internet radio station. Musicians will use streams to play at a given Second Life location. Clubs will often have their own streams that DJs can access to play their set, but sometimes DJs will need to provide their own stream (Shoutcast seems to be the most common provider for this) and the club will then change the parcel settings to play that particular stream.

Teleport: The main means of long-distance travel in Second Life. Is often used as a noun as much as a verb, since the interface is such that one 'offers a teleport' to someone else.

Tier: The common term for the Land Usage Fees charged for mainland. Think of it as a monthly 'property tax.' The first 512 square meters of mainland are free with a Premium membership and then tier increases based on the amount of land you own. Note this is for mainland property--island property is paid for directly to Linden Lab by the owner of the island, and how said owner charges for 'purchase' of land on that island is up to that individual.

Tiny: When used as a noun instead of an adjective, a "Tiny" describes an avatar that combines a very small body shape, numerous attachments and an animation override to become a small creature (or robot, or what have you) of some kind.

Titler: A scripted object, worn as an attachment somewhere around the head, that places hovertext over the avatar, for whatever reason one may want to put some there.

TP: Abbreviation for "Teleport."

Viewer: The program used to access Second Life, much as a web browser allows one to access the World Wide Web. The standard issue viewer can be downloaded from SecondLife.com but there are also other viewers that avies can make use of, some by individual programmers and others created through open source initiatives. A short list can be found by conducting a web search for "Second Life Viewer".

The Highly Opinionated and Utterly Unofficial Second Life FAQ

So what the heck is this Second Life thing, anyway?

Well, the short answer is the one provided on the SecondLife.com website--"Second Life is a 3D online digital world imagined and created by its residents."
The longer answer, well, it borders on a philosophical debate. ("What is the *meaning* of Second Life?")
The medium answer goes something like this--Second Life is the latest iteration of this crazy thing we call The Internet. It is a three-dimensional 'world' that you access online, where you can create content and interact with others. It has its roots in things from the tail end of the 20th century like The Palace (a graphic based chat program), VRML (Virtual Reality Modeling Language--a means of creating 3D environments for people to interact with) and even, to a degree, the text-based MUSHes, MUCKs and MOOs of yore.

So it's, like, a game?

Mmmm, not precisely. (And be careful who you ask that question of, 'cos you're likely to get smacked for asking it.) While there are some similarities to online games like World of Warcraft, in terms of meeting far-flung individuals in a virtual, three-dimensional-rendered space, Second Life doesn't really have a specific goal in terms of levels or quests or missions.

What do you do there?

All kinds of things. You can go to dance clubs to hear DJs spinning or even hear live music being streamed. You can visit elaborate gardens and art galleries. You can surf, race cars or skydive. You can join discussions on things from politics to mysticism. Though, admittedly, the majority of people (according to a recent *New York Times* article) apparently spend the bulk of their time shopping for things to outfit their avatar with.

What's an avatar?

An avatar is the "body" you have when you enter this digital world. It can be anything from Neo in a neon trenchcoat to a pink-haired chick to a winged pony to a watermelon. (And that's just if you Torley Linden (see: wiki.secondlife.com/wiki.user:Torley_Linden) While everyone starts out with a few basic shapes and clothes, over time people start spending Lindens on more elaborate and detailed skin, hair, shapes and clothes.

What are "Lindens"?

The word "Linden (after Linden Lab, the company that runs Second Life) can mean one of two things. It can sometimes refer to an employee of Linden Lab, since the avatars of such employees have the surname of "Linden." (Such as Torley Linden, referenced above.) More often, it refers to the "currency" that one uses to buy and sell things in Second Life--Linden Dollars (L$), which everybody calls "Lindens." For clarity, references to Lindens on this site will almost always be regarding the currency use of the term.

Okay, how do I get Lindens to spend on things?

The easiest way is to just go and buy some. You can set up payment information with a credit card or PayPal account and either buy Lindens inworld (if you need them right away) or buy them via the LindeX (on the Second Life website) from other players. There are also third-party sites that buy and sell Lindens, but proceed with caution--while some are legitimate, others sell Lindens obtained through nefarious means (such as stolen credit card numbers) and people who buy them can end up losing what they bought and getting smited for it.

There are also ways of making Lindens within Second Life.

- If your avatar is new enough, you may be able to take advantage of Money Trees. These are trees that new Residents (less than 30 old, I believe) can collect Lindens from, said Lindens having been donated by other Resis who are feeling generous. However, it's my understanding that you also need to have payment information linked to your account in order to collect, and once you've done that, heck, you might as well drop some cash and buy some anyway.
- A soon-to-be obsolete method is camping, which involves staying in one place (usually in a chair, sometimes in an animation pose that has one dancing, scrubbing the floor, etc.) and being paid one Linden for every so many minutes in place. This technique was used to boost traffic statistics for locations so they would show up higher in the Search function. Linden Lab has recently banned the practice, so any place still using camping chairs probably didn't get the memo yet.

- You can also work jobs in Second Life. Yes, really. Clubs need DJs, clothing designers need models, and strip joints and escort services need . . . well, you get the idea. Breaking your back to get a job in Second Life simply isn't worth it, but if you find something you enjoy doing and find a place willing to throw some Lindens your way to do it, by all means, go for it.
- By the way, upgrading to a Premium Membership currently gives you a L$300 per week stipend.
- And, of course, since you're earning all these Lindens to buy stuff from people, you can get Lindens of your own by making stuff other people will want to buy from you. Some people even manage to make enough Lindens to convert them back into cash.

People make real money doing this?

Some do. Not necessarily very much of it, but it is possible. You can't really expect to make a living at it, though, unless you're dealing in real estate.

Wait, people buy and sell land that doesn't actually exist?

People buy and sell a lot of intangible things, when you think about it. I'm paying a modest amount to maintain my personal website, and that's just information stored on a server. Land in Second Life is much the same thing.

So what do people do with this land?

People in Second Life ("Residents", they call them) build houses, create gardens, open shops--they pretty much shape the world that Second Life is. The only things the nice folks at Linden Lab do is create the land and charge a fee (called "tier") to own it, scaled by how much land you own. What you do with that land is pretty much up to you--you can build on it, change the terrain, rent it out, whatever. You can even buy an entire island, if you have the money, and sublet parcels to other people.

How do you build things? Is it difficult?

Building objects is done within Second Life (or "inworld" as folks round there like to say.) Objects are composed of primitives--"prims"--that can be manipulated and linked together. You can then apply textures to those objects, either obtained inworld or uploaded yourself. Note that prims are, effectively, free, but that each texture upload costs L$10. Once you get the hang of the peculiarities of each prim type--box, sphere, cylinder, and so on--building becomes easier. Prims can also be given certain properties through the magic of LSL.

LSL? What's that?

Linden Scripting Language. LSL is a computer language that allows one to program the behaviors of objects in Second Life. This allows for things like doors that open and close, cars that drive, water that flows and chairs that yell at you (and then give you stuff if you sit down in them and have the right letter in your name.) The syntax is apparently similar to C, so if you know anything about that, you might have an easier time understanding it.

What about clothes? Are those hard to make?

Well, that depends. Anybody can create basic clothes by changing their Appearance settings. You can play with the length and the color and, to a degree, the looseness and save your settings. Ta-da! New outfit.

If you want to make clothes people will actually want to buy, it's a little more complicated than that. You'll need a program that can deal in layers and alpha channels (Photoshop being the best known example) and you'll need the templates that map the coordinates for when a texture is applied to clothing. You can get basic ones from the Second Life Website--some designers have created more detailed ones for use as well. Create a texture in Photoshop, use the alpha channel to create transparency (for things like backless dresses), upload it, create a new clothing item in the Appearance settings and apply the texture. And there you are.

Wow, this can get really complicated, can't it?

Tell me about it. I haven't even said anything about animations.

Okay, what are animations?

I'm so glad you asked! Animations allow your avatar to do things like dance, throw punches, kiss people and even look bored when you're sitting down. You can create them in programs that use the Biovision Hierarchy (BVH) format, such as Poser, but there are a couple of free programs (Avimator and Qavimator) that are specifically designed for Second Life avatars.

How can I learn about this sort of stuff?

There are many tutorials available on the web for people to peruse. You can also find classes in-world, by looking them up on the Events Calendar in your user area on the Second Life website.

What if you don't want to make things?

Then you can buy them from the various hard-working Residents of Second Life who have gone and made things for you to enjoy.

Okay, how do I sign up? Does it cost anything?

Signing up is free. A paid membership is optional--it provides things like the stipend, mentioned above, the right to buy land (though you can sublet from an Island owner without a membership) and marginally better technical support.

Before you sign up, though, if you have gone straight to this back page I advise you start at the beginning and read all of the information in this guide.

Trust me on this one!

www.ingramcontent.com/pod-product-compliance
Lightning Source LLC
Chambersburg PA
CBHW060933050326
40689CB00013B/3075